THE VOICE IN THE HEADPHONES

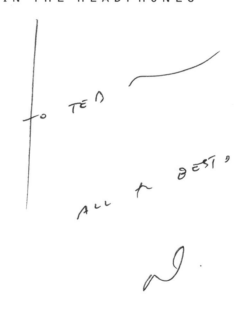

THE VOICE IN THE HEADPHONES

DAVID GRUBBS

DUKE UNIVERSITY PRESS *Durham and London* 2020

© 2020 DUKE UNIVERSITY PRESS

All rights reserved

Printed in the United States of America on
acid-free paper ∞

Designed by Matthew Tauch

Typeset in Garamond Premier Pro
by Copperline Books

Library of Congress Cataloging-in-Publication Data
Names: Grubbs, David, [date] author.
Title: The voice in the headphones / David Grubbs.
Description: Durham : Duke University Press, 2020.
Identifiers: LCCN 2019032494 (print)
LCCN 2019032495 (ebook)
ISBN 9781478007685 (hardcover : acid-free paper)
ISBN 9781478008132 (paperback : acid-free paper)
ISBN 9781478009092 (ebook)
Subjects: LCSH: Sound recordings—Production and
direction—Poetry. | Avant-garde (Music)
Classification: LCC PS3557. R76 V65 2020 (print)
LCC PS3557. R76 (ebook)
DDC 811/.54—dc23
LC record available at https://lccn.loc.gov/2019032494
LC ebook record available at https://lccn.loc.gov/2019032495

Cover art: Josiah McElheny, *Three Screens for Looking
at Abstraction* (detail, in homage to Walter Ruttmann),
2012. Aluminum, low-iron mirror, projection cloth, film
transferred to video (variable program), video projectors
with stands, wood, and metal hardware, dimensions variable.
Photograph by Mark Steele.

The one thing I like about popular music is that they record it. They record it, record it, record it, record it! The astute producer cuts out the magic from the different tapes (*laughter*), and puts them in a certain order and gets the whole piece.

—ROBERT ASHLEY

THE VOICE IN THE HEADPHONES

The voice in the headphones says, "You're rolling"

followed by ten seconds of line-hum silence, an intercom-like click, and the reminder "You're still rolling."

One rolls. Will roll. Will still roll, will break the seal

on another workday at the former Skylight Magnetic Re-cording Services, now just Skylight Recording. Think Tues-day or Wednesday, perpetual charmed workday, and try to pierce the headspace

of the person on the other side of the glass, the one who rolls tape. Who rolled tape when tape exclusively rolled. The one who monitors the virtual tape transport, who with compe-tent diffuse

concentration watches software fader-representations fly, who in spite of fatigue keeps a gentle controlling hand on the ses-sion, driving commercial freight bumper to bumper, night after night into morning after morning.

Skylight rents tape

by the reel. Envision the various storage spaces along the Gowanus Canal and all the reels of two-inch tape moldering inside. At one time they were sourced from a dealer opposite Green-Wood Cemetery, the last tape and recording media one-stop hunkered among retailers of headstones and memorial monuments. Admit to the temptation to pulp those reels. The doctrine of attractive nuisance states that sometime in the future a person unknown to you will try their hand at improving upon mixes that you made as a very young and confident person, and so dumping sites beckon.

Roll rented tape

———

to savor the full stop of the tape transport as it slams like a circuit breaker. Relish the precursor, pre-flashing-cursor, antecedent to digital media's attendant cursor, the newly internalized minute and mile marker

less pulsing than metro-

noming beneath eyelids. The end of a reel of two-inch tape forcefully punctuates. Engage the high-speed rewind, gun it in the straightaway, and steel yourself as the end of the reel flaps insanely. Point a microphone at the acoustic event of the tape machine's possession, but do it quickly before the tantrum passes, before the thing completely shreds. Record ten or twenty seconds of it, an almost unbearably long take, and then multitrack multiple passes of however many slaps per second. Fade in on the unfortunate scene.

It snowed nearly a foot last night.

Winter palace. The world outside the studio

that much more muted. Hard to ignore such symmetry.

Rent tape to warm things up. Rent tape to militate against unseemly sharpness, to denature digital, and hail the hoary apparition of the best worst sound system you know intimately. Stand down, pixel.

Rent tape to track the snake.

Loop the snake escaping and snake the loop reentering the machine. Repeat beyond necessary. Maintain the tape loop's tension with mic stands as macro capstan shafts, and send around the perimeter of the control room this compendium of a dozen perspectives on the flapping of the end of a reel of tape, a flustered aviary of. Roll at fifteen inches per second and then seven and a half and still slower. Inch it forward by hand, rock it back and forth. Send it down an octave and more while rippling the surface with slight tugs and flocking salutations.

First-person plural feedback plunges

through glass. At the far end of the live room, sliding doors
open onto an unbroken surface of snowy hillside. For the
musician preparing to do a take, it's a landscape more prompt
than score, more distraction than prompt.

Exceptional quilt-like quiet awaits indices

Intercom click. Stumble off

the high dive. Gravity's aide-de-plummet—arm, wrist, hand
—falls. Guillotine strikes string, and string survives. With
this sounding, the hum in the headphones is revealed as
nothing but haze, merest medium lacking substance to sup-
port the weight of an instrument, the guitar's attack dispel-
ling sheer folds.

The emptiness says I'm listening.

Still rolling.

The aural tint that bespoke diagnostic seashell to which heart-beats heel has been replaced by a surround of self-inflicted blare inside tight headphones. It's ten in the morning, and this is the first take of the day.

Cotton to the tremble of the tubes.

Electronic modulation drops the pitch of the lowest string more than four octaves. What's less heard than felt to resonate the cheekbones is the difference in frequency between fretted note and dialed-in reference tone. The illusion is that of a stringed instrument

with a neck many times as long, invisibly suspended so that the operator can circle around and zero in on that fingernail's breadth bull's-eye. Strings of cable-like thickness register and massively amplify tectonic tremor, a differential rumble

falls to its knees, and the mind is welcome to attend to the discontinuous chatter of filament rattle. Distracted thought plumbs excluded muddle, that buffer between extremes of buzzing glass and amplified-string excitation.

Headphones respire at humming-

bird

tempo. The left index finger pulls this first pitch sharp so that the difference tone correspondingly drops; it falls below the range of hearing, lies supine, puddles, and then just as suddenly rebounds, gathering force as it regains form. Everything changes in the relaxing of a finger and the prompt, unexpected return to pitch that completes the day's inaugural splash of sound. Let's hope we've been rolling. The return to pitch transports the difference tone from unseen underworld to floodlit field of play where it resounds with fretted note and glass crown.

A second attack, this time an open string, sends the phantom tone that much higher, settling as it cools, the two sounds coming to rest in consonance. To think of the years the musician spent avoiding the sound of an open string. After a pause, a twist of the tuning machine breaks the bond and shatters the concord. This precise splitting of tones summons feedback in flickers

illuminates by strobe the rotation of an owl's neck. It pierces backdrop and baffle with pinholes of painful brightness, and then the rehearsal tape arrives.

The rehearsal tape flies in via a twenty-year-old cassette discovered several days ago in a storage-space shoebox. When it appears with calculated abruptness in the musician's headphones, it suggests a slowed recording of tennis-shoe mallets inside a clothes-dryer drum. Listen for the roars and cries of Skull Island elephants

and tigers. The tape dates back to an invitation two decades before to escape the city for several days, bad times abounding, and the opportunity to complete a batch of songs. At that juncture they were less songs than four or five stretches of differing terrain for guitar or piano, but promisingly separable; they could be cultivated to grow apart.

He took along a cassette for a weekend of words.

Pack the boombox in the trunk.

Song lyrics for the musician two decades earlier came awkwardly coiled, not to be untangled but cut into shorter lengths for the gnarl to relax. Begin by matching words with a musical patch of ground and then let the scissors have at; allow eraser or strikethrough or sequence of carefully subtractive recopyings to skew ever shorter. Praise phrases that float

and praise phrases clumping and coordinating to round off such writings. At the end of the four-hour drive, hungry to start work, the first hint that something was awry was that the cassette needed to be rewound.

———

Place the boombox atop pine needles

on the forest floor. It rewinds contentedly. The tape must have played itself to the end of the side by accident. A thunk and futile straining signals the completed rewind, press play

then the past comes back wrong—horribly so, unflowingly slow. The tape rolls, batteries beacon bright, and the past rumbles out incognito with an aura of distant spelunking, the carving of caverns. Put an ear to the ground to inspect the instinctively mistrusted sound.

Headphones stethoscopically confirm that the sound is coming from within the trunk. That it came from within the trunk, was at one time heard inside the trunk, machine-heard and captured. Something shifted and the boombox began to record; a torque or fishtail must have started it rolling in the bowels of the mobile unit. What's playing back, what's plaguing this small clearing in the forest appears to be basic boring frictionless highway, not the stop and go of leaving the city on a Friday afternoon. Long-game literalism. The claustrophobe

on the open road, overwriting. Skree it

forward however many minutes and it's manifestly the same, the drone of the inadvertently documented, and the musician's task for the weekend remains that of matching words to it, whatever it has become.

The past arrives in the musician's headphones in the form
of a kidnapped cassette from twenty years prior that crashes
the take, and here we are again reporting live from inside the
trunk. For the record, the jury never returned its verdict on
whether present sliced open spews future. Insert your arm
up to the elbow to touch the time of day. The past cuts in to
dance

and it seems a long separation. File under

another future no one wanted.

On this winter morning, pitch modulated performance and concrete sound fuse electronically and jointly counter-mand years of weekends of words and attempts at song. Stay and rumble awhile

up the snowy hill and back with minimal alteration to its surface. Project yourself into the view, there's nowhere else to be, and let it carom back to the performance; allow it to impress itself

upon the take. Enmesh yourself in a music where it's nearly impossible to take a wrong step. It's understood that one can always fuck it up—every soul has a genius for doing wrong. But the present situation demands only that you place one foot in front of the other.

A music like walking.

A music as peculiar as walking.

Walking out the sliding door and up the hill

.

A music like a walk in the snow.

A music like the sound of a walk in the snow.

A music regulated by breath during a walk in the snow

.

A music like walking atop the snow.

A music like snowshoes, for scampering across.

A music for hiding and haring across

.

A music to take with you over the mountain.

A music that takes you over the mountain.

Denuded succession and air

congeals to rime. Defines blurred cold friction.

Take a drag through the snow. The fog freezes and a stream sounds beneath the faint outline of a bridge. Two hundred shades of white. When you're confident that the time has come, the decision is yours to reverse course. A music obscured by scrim, a music that ceases to reflect readiness. Before you're completely frozen

turn this ship around, one foot after another. With a nagging sense of detour, with continued detour and perpetual listing aim for the studio.

Find the precise spot at which it ceases to be

a journey outward, the point where the tether most power-fully strains. A sudden perimeter, an echoed antipode. At-tune yourself to that location your body knows to be the most distant and most demanding, and plot your return from the furthest farthest. How deeply can you sleep when you know you must be leaving soon?

The streetlights extinguished, the sun not up.

Bring the figure to a close.

Bring the first take of the morning to completion with a slow shade into silence. The sounds from within the trunk have long since faded out, the strings have been slackened, the array of slide implements scattered on the studio floor, the amplifier tubes stilled. There's only the deafened dampened hum in one's head.

Raise hand to stop tape.

Not using tape. Where did the engineer go?

Ten seconds later he's back in the control room with a fresh cup of coffee. Click, room tone: "Were you happy with that?" Three additional figures glide in, also cupping large steaming mugs. The musician experiences a disorienting recognition of familiar faces. Actually: the Familiar Faces, one and the same, chief among a handful of signature groups from the previous decade to whom, in the opinion of pockets of fans, the middle of the country briefly belonged. It was all starting to happen, it was a definite go, stars and planets aligned, and then it didn't. Not really. It's hard to say

and has everything to do with who's listening. The group consists of a brother, a sister, and a cousin, the last of whom is less likely a blood relative than an ostentatiously handsome excuse for a mediating multi-instrumentalist never appearing in the publishing credits, the brooding iconic Face.

The guitar is gently placed on its stand, the headphones jettisoned, cables navigated, and a path to the control room discovered for a round of unanticipated hometown embraces. The musician had imagined a more solitary morning, especially with an engineer whom it will take time to learn to read. It could be enlightened distance

it could be the middle of the week. The Familiar Faces forcefully and famously imploded a decade earlier; whether or not you care about their music, the recent documentary about them fascinates with family dynamics and reticent, oddly formulated stabs at accounting for collective creation in a last sliver of time

before everything was caught on video. The Familiar Faces finished their top-secret session in the adjoining studio around sunrise, by which it's understood that the effort was abandoned.

The revelation of the client's identity explains the use of a code name—"Ringo"—on the locked door of Studio A. It's unclear whether any of the three poker Faces in immediate retrospect think the reunion was anything but a misfire.

The Familiar Faces seem puzzled by what's happening in Studio B. Their presence is an index of how far peers can drift in two decades of music-making, and how broad the results can be even as the authorizing impulse was the same: post-hardcore, post-punk, teenage and generational stylistic straightjacketing shed and musicians diverging in outward flux. Back then who would have identified as a musician? Hindsight can be impossibly wrong. "Do you want to try that again?" asks the engineer. Nope. "Do you want to listen back?" Negatory.

The Familiar Faces politely take it all in.

Small talk yields negligible intel on the Familiar Faces' reunion.

Few facts are volunteered. They've formally relinquished Studio A and the engineer has been dismissed. The musician can't make out whether the group arrived at Skylight Recording with a raft of new compositions, whether they intended to write in the studio, or what their method might have been. What's certain is that over refilled mugs of coffee there's relief at again splintering the triangle of their devising. A minimum of eye contact passes among group members, now maybe nonmembers

with no attempt to downplay their escapist curiosity about the goings-on in Studio B. They scent the air with questions from the most nuts-and-bolts to the unanswerably hypothetical as each Face inches closer to offering her or his skills. Who bailed

---

on this or the previous effort to reconvene the group, a week of anxious rehearsals in anticipation of what would have been reverently welcomed by those who weren't able to witness the first go-round?

They were children then, but soon to escape the orbit of the pit, the gyre of slamming and stage diving and soundtracking the ninety-second riot. From the word one-two-three-four it was the trio of Brother and Sister in the frontline, spiked hair, just starting high school, and Cousin behind the kit, mastering and elevating the generic American thrash beat after a scant few tries. Parents in cars outside gigs

killed entire evenings talking about who knows what. At their first show a frisbeed metal trashcan lid flew above the audience and demolished Cousin's cymbals. They were still sprouts the summer it all went elastic and they began to hone a more private musical language. Hand me your instrument, you take mine.

Everyone became buoyant

falling and rising in the aquarium

the smallest room in the house

,

the tiny room where they set up their gear

at your party, at anyone's party—the better to

approximate the dimensions of the rehearsal space.

It was a simple idea: always playing in the same room. No additional amplification was required, and the trio set up so that they faced one another, backs to the audience, aloof

at the heart of the thrumming

house. Somehow the Familiar Faces' m.o. as three individuals collectively turned inward grew all wrong. If on this snowed-in morning they no longer engage one another with anything like the kinship or trust or demonstrable appreciation that once colored their cryptic bond it isn't because they've moved on to new partnerships. In the absence of group sentiment, it's unclear what's taken its place.

The first of the Familiar Faces' two farewell videos from a decade earlier consists of a simple line dance shot in black and white in a continuous three-minute take at the Wicker Park bar that doubled as their office. Six hands clap!

Three steps to the right, clap! Three steps to the left, same! Sister occupies the middle with a fedora tipped over her forehead, ponytail tied with a dark ribbon. The trio takes two steps forward with fingers snapping, turns ninety degrees to the right, and hits the downbeat with a forceful hop. There's a three-beat rest of twitchy anticipation and gathering steam, a right-leg sweep and thrust of the right hand resulting in a shoulder dip, a left-leg sweep and concomitant gesture, another right-leg sweep, two steps forward into a ninety-degree twist to the right, and a hop that allows the pattern to start again.

The mix is such that handclaps and footsteps and shuffling sounds frequently obscure the piece of music that the video is supposed to advertise. On several occasions the underlying musical track cuts out entirely and all that remains is the sound of the trio huffing their way through the dance. In one instance the diegetic barroom sound is replaced by Sister's voiceover:

———

When Rudolph Valentino died
Three steps to the right, silent clap

the studio yanked his films
three steps to the left, ditto

thinking to bury them alongside the star
two steps forward with soundless snaps

lest their ghoulish profiteering permanently alienate movie-goers.
and a furious hop in which the dancers are proudly out of sync.

Another ninety-degree turn. The three participants' relationship to the dance shifts like shadows cast by clouds, and that's the story the video tells. Commitment is fleeting, surging in isolated steps and stomps. Handsome tall Cousin, at far right and closest to the camera, comes across as the most natural of the bunch. It's a splendid act, and he's the first to drop out and exit the frame. Who's next? Brother sweatily shakes it in a slept-in v-neck sweater, cigarette expertly managed. Let him complete another repetition of the pattern, and the subsequent ninety-degree turn becomes his opportunity to bow out.

Sister continues by herself, borderline-ecstatic without these lugs, giddy to be going it alone. She's the sole survivor. Then boredom overtakes her, the grin crumbles, and the clip ends.

The Familiar Faces' final video features the trio taking on New York City. The song's three-line verses lend themselves to an intercutting between three storylines in which each member of the group struggles to make it to the venue in time for the show. Sister flies into Newark, Brother into JFK, Cousin into LaGuardia. Numerous delays are averted; police cruisers chase the "L" train out Milwaukee Avenue, benches and suitcases are hurdled in O'Hare, and somehow each band member arrives on time at one of the three New York airports. At the baggage claim, large DON'T RIDE WITH THESE GUYS posters are visible over the shoulders of the out-of-focus band members. The sign depicts two unlicensed drivers: the loutish haranguing white guy with a cigar and herringbone flat-top cap and the perhaps South Asian man in a rumpled white shirt and loosened tie.

As the Familiar Faces exit their respective airports into the blinding day of the sold-out concert, the two villains of DON'T RIDE WITH fame make their cameos, appearing curbside and welcoming Brother and Cousin as unwitting fares.

Sister takes the bus.

———

The three storylines picture the three passengers beholden to the same reverie as the sun sets over Manhattan.

Sister is the first to arrive at the well-known downtown music venue. She squints at her wristwatch, triggering a split screen in which Brother and Cousin both fail to notice that their drivers are following signs to Staten Island. There's a moment in which the two unlicensed cabs come to a halt side by side in traffic on the Verrazano Bridge — a flash of eye contact connects the drivers — but neither passenger notices the other. Their dreaming is interrupted only when the stars of the DON'T RIDE WITH campaign, actors whose careers would be jump-started by this video, pull up to the garbage dump, hustle their fares out of the respective cars, and execute each with a shot to the back of the head. The two lifeless bodies are given a push and sent rolling down steep opposing slopes.

The split screen resolves into a single frame as the corpses gently collide at the bottom of the landfill. Sister checks her watch one last time before striding onstage.

———

The first take of the day always brings the musician back to a first take from a decade earlier, his and his friends' initial step outside of a more conventionally organized band, a shift in which the rhythm section began to reimagine its duties.

On that particular morning there was a drummer behind what you would recognize as a drum kit, and for seven minutes or so he sat inaudibly smoking a cigarette. At the end of the piece, as it counted down its closing seconds, the drummer decided to hazard a slight bit of rumbling noise, floor-tom swells with a little nonmetrical kick-drum lub-dubbing, and several flicks of brushes landing near the bell of the ride cymbal.

It was a piece of recorded music

in that the players did their best to consider the listener at home wondering what could be occupying the drummer for seven irretrievable minutes. What's so important about a punch-card

pattern of arpeggios and asymmetries that it necessitates removing a stellar performer from the musical workforce? The core of the spare arrangement was a walking bassline transposed to an otherwise affectless Fender guitar, the sound of Corona, California capoed at the ninth fret so that open strings assume the upper-range unfamiliarity of a countertenor.

That doesn't answer your question. The musician recalls listening to this first playback of the day sprawled on a stiff Persian carpet at the still center of a spinning public access studio, trying to hold it together. He'd sensed at the conclusion of the take that this would be the one—everyone knew it—that it answered the call and should not be second-guessed. Performers toggle into listeners awaiting the recognition that justice has been done

———

and it was agony.

From the first, the playback confirmed that they had handled the piece at an impossibly slow tempo, and that this would make for brutal listening even lying down. Pinned to the carpet, he felt a need to thrash wildly in protest. His vertigo was triggered by the dispiriting music as presentiment of a painfully long day: the lock-in. What could be going through the drummer's head during this interminable series of rests when at any moment he could dive in and save his flailing bandmates?

Why wouldn't you correct a friend

———

who persists in what's objectively wrong?

It had been agreed: no more bludgeoning. The unilateral disarmament that the group internally negotiated over the previous year felt like a breakthrough. It was premised on a vague but nonetheless shared idea among the members about music on a human scale. It would be apartment music, living-room music. Respect-your-neighbors music. It was to be morning, afternoon, and evening music—flexible and adaptive—in which acoustic and electric instruments find equal footing, music premised on a one-to-one scale and the insight that it's better to sing in the silences. But as this enervating playback of the first take of the day wound its way toward a conclusion

who'd be fool enough to speak first?

Skip ahead a few months. By then the take will strike the musician as moving at an effortless clip, a nuanced reading that picks up the tempo at just the right moments, indecision recast as skillful navigation and the artful handling of one transition after the next—performance approaching an ideal of continuous transition.

Maybe slower next time, says the affirmation

of breeze and skin.

The musician seats himself at the organ.

Applying himself to the task of adding layers to this same piece of music—today's work consists of a single piece—his plan is to record pitches one at a time in order to have the ability to shape discrete volume contours within clusters and dense voicings. To handle the instrument so that it stretches its legs, so it approximates

tarantula, the striking anatomy of. Remind us again what happens when the animal loses a leg, we blocked that image. The offensive posture of. Strike key and depress prey. Each pitch within the cluster throbs autonomously, respires in slow-bursting beats of feigned wooziness.

Start at the far left of the footboard. Record five minutes of examples of volume swells, subsequent passes overdubbed with headphones on, monitoring to what end it's not entirely clear. To seed the cloud. To time the swells, to counterbalance. Within antiphonal listening

to focus on beating patterns based on the speeds of individual tone wheels, the agreement of tone wheel and magnetic pickup. To manage with the fewest but most musical hiccups the lengthening of the draw bar. Best to get with the math: eight marks the prime, eight states the fundamental. Eight legs, and you can always grow a replacement or restart the take. Dividing by two doubles the frequency, dividing once again sends it two octaves aloft. Eight to four to two to

one, remembering that this is a single jostling group of overtones among many. A détente is heard to hold. Blend octaves, perfectly reanimated fourths, and a thickening firmament of fifths. As the full complement of cylinders engages, the Leslie speaker whirls its unheeded alarm of smaller and smaller intervals and shorter and shorter microintervallic spans, less shield than echo-texture to emotion less exoskeleton than strutting bones

of the beast. Skepticism toward mere measurement in a se-
quence of swells successfully resolves itself, no matter the
layers or legs, no matter the difficult hoisting and balancing
of the carapace. Inharmonic synthesis distresses itself from
within; pickups are all ears and don't scruple at the content
of their conveyances, least of all this insane spinning speaker
town-crying

fingertips cresting waterfall.

Eight lines winnow with each pass shading a touch

quieter. There's always less to say.

Always less to

Eight passes on the organ suffice for a spectrogram

of dissociated spiderly gait. The musician makes the most of the quasi-downtime of his simple task—one overdub after the next—to meditate on his surroundings in Studio B. What's the oldest artifact in its display of music memorabilia and stoner outsider art? Disassemble the live room

and sort its contents chronologically. Next to the bank of light switches and dimmers is a scotch-taped selection of yellowing gross-out newspaper clippings that dates back thirty years: Mud Man Captured, Astro-Nut Love Triangle. The room's sedimentary layers correlate to recognizable signposts in pop-music aesthetics, never swept out and begun again but built around, allowed to ossify. Remain in shadow.

The live room's sliding glass doors frame the previous evening's snowfall, but at other times of the year they open onto a stream stocked with trout. The glass doors are flanked by dyed and spray-painted wall hangings, nicotine-cured sagging bedsheets with silver and gray clouds frugging at eye level.

Parachutists in red silhouette descend in diagonal

formation against a lozenge-patterned sky of turquoise and military drab. Blitzkrieg, argyle: scheißegal. Four freestanding acoustic baffles sport a similarly hallucinatory aerial dogfight theme. Purple fronds and eye-pocked peacock feathers dispel japoniste cloud wisps and provide cover for hiding and seeking upside-down biplanes in an acid-yellow sky.

A coat of white paint atop uneven floorboards long ago lost the battle to biker boots, cowboy boots, kick-drum spurs, and backbreaking gear whether dragged or on wheels. A trinity of frankensteined guitars

hangs from a wall-mounted rack in an alcove fashioned from African textiles. Every inch of the room's lone concrete pillar is covered with signatures, scatological and pornographic doodles, and hand-drawn band logos with the least known the largest. The Möbius strips of band names attest to years spent in practice rooms: Hippo Blood, Ugly Daylight, People Who Work for the Witch, Sadie Is a Snitch, Scrape-

grace, Wit of the Basket Case, Bob Hopeless, Typhoid Raúl, the Mung, the Sneers, the Wojciks, the Punji Sticks, the Educated Thrushes, Moonfeather, Pennsyltucky, the Madmen from Massachusetts, the Amoral Higher Ground, Sir Edgar and the Pugs, Potentates and Impresarios, Krankenhaus, Waschbär 69, Shit the Bed. A stack of amplifiers patriotically obscures an inverted U.S. flag. Silver Mardi Gras and commedia masks and feather boas of many colors encircle a mirror tagged with a haiku stenciled in white spray paint. The vocal booth doubles as tape vault and toolshed.

Headspace fills to overflowing as the musician nears an endgame of organ overdubs. Oxygen has long since been sucked out of the substance. Eight organ lines radiate as edges amplified into interference patterns. Noise in the channel

scrambles ground control—must assume we're still rolling—and the spray-painted aerial duelists are forced to improvise as they square off, flock of red versus panoply of pink in interpenetrating chevrons, close values

auguring close conflict. Eight lines correspond to parachute string lines terminating in sound-baffling canopies. Each overdub lands a bit more softly than the last, each less distinct and more forgiving. Cue a final billow of fabric.

Land in the vicinity of horizon. Remove headphones

and return to the base. The control room, the engineer's do-
main, shares none of the patchwork visual disposition of Stu-
dio B's guileless, souvenir-strewn live room where for years
even the most adolescent musicians have been encouraged to
leave their mark. The control room by contrast announces
itself as a secure viewing area: the observation side of one-way
glass from which the lab coats keep tabs on their test subjects.
At regular intervals the engineer flips on a diminutive light
therapy lamp that projects concentrated blue sky at him

and at him alone. The costly, obscenely veined rosewood slats
that line the control-room walls bespeak a pendulum return,
more precisely a change of ownership, from the DIY hippie
décor of the live room to a more recent imperative to astound
the client with immense wall-recessed conversation-starter
speakers that are rarely used and give little hint how a record-
ing might sound outside of this environment.

When standing in the control room and facing the double-paned glass, one senses the slight outward bow of the resonator walls, intuits floor plans inscribing triangle atop flipped, attenuated triangle

within the control room's implied pentagonal shape. The couch at the back is the classic counterindicated spot for close listening. This is where the space shades into bass trap, particularly for the prone listener with ears buried among pillows and exhibiting signs of exhaustion or defeat.

The musician flops face down on the sofa.

While the musician had been working on organ overdubs, the Familiar Faces helped themselves to a closetful of antiquated drum machines resembling vintage dictaphones, answering machines, and toy telephone switchboards. All three Faces wear headphones and operate in distinct, cut-off spheres of electronic-instrument research

or threefold parallel play featuring Rhythm Ace, Mini Pops, and Donca-Matic, with Eko ComputeRhythm at the ready. Cribbing the musician's technique of recording individual tones with an ear toward maximum compositional flexibility, each Face focuses on subdividing the functions of these earliest mechanized rhythm devices, whether by isolating voices—weird term for white-noise

blasts shaped by amplitude envelopes—through the removal of unwanted frequency bands or by dumping test firings into a sampler to refashion troglodyte two-steps as lustrous fractals. Something has begun

to smolder. The musician is loath to turn over too much of the session to the three Faces, each of whom gives the impression of having all the time in the world and a hunger for distraction. He gives them a firm twenty minutes to get their act together and record as a trio a single real-time overdub of synthesized percussion. A few constructive words and phrases are shared among Brother, Sister, and Cousin, and the musician's Solomonic cutting to the chase appears to have been the correct impulse.

The trio has a question. Is there a score?

———

The musician's written materials consist of a single page in which the names of pitches appear in straight lines and forty-five degree parenthetical offshoots with the calligraphic subtlety of Proto-Norse. Writing bleeds

to the page's edges in rows of letters divided by rows of letters and still further interleaved, notational threads distinguishable only by virtue of differing shades of ink and legibility. The name of every fourth or fifth note is alternately circled or underscored in pencil—a number of colored pencils clustered within an unfortunately close range of hues—not to mention straight and curving arrows, cross outs, and twice-versus three-times underscored Xs, markings that given a patient interpreter and sufficient time might emerge as complex regularities representing polyrhythms.

The Familiar Faces genuinely would like to understand.

It's unclear what's sequence

what's simultaneity

what's to hang

what's to

twist

,

much less what's instructed, what's encouraged, what's understood, what's tacitly permitted, and where one flies solo. At what point does a branching path represent separate phrases, and how might these phrases be distributed among members of an ensemble? These and similar details should be easy to explain to well-intentioned collaborators, and yet the Faces have stumbled into an area in which the musician is prone to panic.

Take it as compendium, stocked stream, orchard, or vale, and the fact that the page is such an overwritten mess is immaterial, apologies. The musician starts and stops and points and hums

a dissonant tune that doesn't repeat. He describes with an awkward combination of words and eight wiggling fingers spider legs and densely voiced, precisely tuned drones. There's conspiratorial talk of sounds that originate in the ear. The ways in which this single page of handwritten notation might be parsed remain very much up for grabs, its author unable to settle on an explanation or even a place to begin, and so the question languishes and the trio returns to their drum machines.

For what might be the last time the Familiar Faces take their places in the group's signature inward-facing triangle, each responding to a different headphone mix.

Cousin carpet-rides the up- and downdrafts of organ over-dubs, Sister faces the full-frequency extremes of rise-and-shine noise guitar, and Brother meditates upon lonely hours cruising the interstate

in the trunk of a car. The three-sided electronic drum circle privileges whiplash shifts between interior monologue, par-liamentary debate, grade-school drum line, and Hell Night riot. An overturned police car burns to the ticking of non-synchronous clocks.

Three pulses drift, split

differences, briefly align, recon-

noiter, part without accusation or recrimination

dut dut dut

          pok   pok dut

       dut **dut**   **pok** pok

  dut

dut pok

pok **pok** pok

pok dut   dut

dut   dut dut **pok**

dut dut   **dut**   pok

                    pok

                                        pok

                    dut dut **pok**   **pok**

                              dut

dut dut dut

pok **pok** pok   pok **dut**

dut dut **pok** dut dut **dut** pok dut pok

dut pok dut dut **pok** dut **pok**

The musician must have drifted to sleep early in the take.

On waking he reads the clear satisfaction in all three Faces, and it provides the jolt of energy he needs to rise from the sofa and banish the thought of a more substantial nap. Even the engineer concurs that this first-take fracturing of the timekeeping function is for the ages and so the clock

strikes lunch. It's common knowledge among clients of the studio that the engineer's cooking skills are essential to the Skylight experience. With an enthusiasm sometimes lacking in his other responsibilities the engineer fetches and with sudden brio snaps open five vintage TV trays. The four musicians find themselves transported back to rule-bending dinners in front of the television during visits to grandparents and aunts and uncles long since deceased.

Five hot conical covered dishes arrive with today's lunch: the engineer's first attempt at a vegetarian cassoulet. He takes pleasure in explaining that the white beans are flavored by a mixture of crimini mushrooms, acorn squash, parsnips, carrots, leeks, and onions so that there's no need for meat. An improbable roux pulls it together. While everyone waits for the meal to cool, the engineer prepares the studio for his favorite parlor game.

The engineer had a habit for a brief, idyllic stretch in the 1990s of liberating unclaimed backup copies of 24-track tapes marked for destruction at an especially cavalier high-end studio. In most cases he wiped the tapes and offered them free of charge to musicians for whom not having to purchase a new reel was a significant windfall. But the contents of some of these tapes were too familiar and consequently too strange to be erased, hence this lunchtime game of the multi-track master edition of *Name That Tune*. As the clients enjoy their white bean stew, the engineer gives the fallow Studer 24-track machine a quick diagnostic exam, nothing seriously wrong, and cues up the mystery reel.

A threading of the broad magnetic needle and thud of the play button kicks into gear venerable hypnotic blacksnaking and everyone shuts up good. The presentation starts with an isolated track.

An approximation of piano chimes coldly. It must have been an early digital effort, a preset straight out of the box. The precise regularity of its attacks conveys rote insistence, and it's difficult to stay focused on the part as it rocks back and forth between suspended chords in a robotic vamp. There's little possibility of identifying the song on the basis of this minimal musical content, but its brittle timbre and the fact that it was recorded to tape narrow the time frame. Is this a song we've heard before?

It was definitely in the top ten, might have been number one. The four contestants, now invested in the competition, meditate deeply on the digital piano part. The eighties-nineties cusp can be tricky. As the one-minute mark arrives, a not-unexpected upward modulation rings a distant if unnamable bell, but no one hazards a guess.

———

Back to the top. The engineer mutes the piano

and the ball disappears beneath one of three inverted cups. In its place is a diaphanous shroud of synthesizer standing in for orchestral strings. It's a binding agent, a phantom substance within which the piano lies silently twitching. Responding to a collective groan, the engineer opens another channel and fades in a triumphant motif on a sampled oboe. No air was disturbed in the making of—

it entwines dissonantly with the incoming Skype.

Right back at ya, and a happy new year to you as well. It's going, it's definitely going. I can catch you up, but for now you need to get in on the game. We're just finishing lunch and trying to identify this song one element at a time. Eighties-nineties. I have faith that you'll figure it out.

Everyone wave, this is the filmmaker.

As the song starts to fluoresce at the one-minute mark, the engineer again stops the tape and rewinds. The piece is next presented in the form of a trio of digital piano, orchestral-strings synth, and Wagnerian forest-journey sampled oboe. With flawless timing—clearly he's practiced this—the engineer drops into the mix a palm-muted rope-a-dope of chorused electric guitar and the imaginary scene shifts to a fitness club. Is this a load-bearing part of the puzzle? Can we buy another track?

———

This time the guitar workout is accompanied by a thick electric bass, fret buzz and all, struggling to catch up with the beat. In this otherwise airless context it brings a winningly louche sloppiness. The patient had flatlined, and then to everyone's surprise the EEG began to boogie. Titles start to form on the contestants' tongues, and the filmmaker, via Skype, appears closest to solving the puzzle. At 1:09 — those make-or-break additional nine seconds — the engineer permits the contestants to hear the shocking crack

of a snare and then hits stop and rewinds amid vociferous booing. We want a vocal! Digital piano vamp, string-synth gauze, pompous freeze-dried oboe, Nautilus-machine guitar, sketchily sight-read bass part

and within a fraction of a second after unmuting the vocal track — the grand reveal — each of the contestants not only recognizes the singer but also the song, the both so thunderingly familiar that no one shouts out the answer.

———

It sounds completely amazing. This should have been an Olympic anthem. It sounds like five finalists for a new Olympic anthem on top of one another. The mega-anthem of five finalists written by the world's greatest AI programs. The hyper-anthem. I'm getting chills. I'm loving every second of this, I'm starting to cry. I thought the whole exercise was a cynical demonstration of recording studio means-ends rationality, a pedantic lesson in how little some extremely successful folks give a shit, or how some folks become successful by knowing when not to give a shit, and how listeners turn a blind eye to both. All those tracks by themselves sound positively rinky-dink, and you put 'em together, and damn! That was some magic trick. Is it the voice? Is it the singing? What makes it all snap into place? Here we were laughing like a bunch of buffoons, just dying, and then it all comes together so beautifully, and what can you say? That there's an art to the mix, that there's an art to the selection and cultivation of materials, especially those that sound like garbage. Here's a singer whose name is synonymous with squandered talent. That's the party line among the generation of rock critics that started using letter grades. I'm giving this one an A, even if I'm years late in turning in the grade. The skewering of belle-lettristic pretenses was a gag, but it hardened into something vile. I'm pretty sure this song came out in 1989, but you wouldn't say that it played a part in the opening of the Berlin Wall and the re-unification, or in Tiananmen Square. It's part and parcel of, for better or worse, the sound of, one of a tremendous number of sounds of, I mean *squandered* bespeaks expectations, and whose were those, really? Have you ever been so fortunate as to have someone, a wise someone, accuse *you* of squandering your talent? Since when does what you might theoretically produce somewhere down the line become part of the public good, the public trust, and need to be administered as such? We were laughing our asses off and then didn't we shut up? I dare say you'd be in Studio A if you hadn't squandered your talent. Don't act like I'm the first to tell you this. Do they even let you see what's going on in Studio A? I'm going to start calling you the Squanderer so that everyone thinks you have an immense talent. You'll thank me for this. If you're stuck in the Studio Bs of the world it's not because at one time you weren't regarded as a serious talent, but because you squandered it. I'll do what I can to see you become this generation's standard bearer for squandering it. Hang your head, Squanderer. You'll never darken the doorway of Studio A, and even the gig of scoring this film isn't yours alone. That's no strike against you because no one got that gig, and I'm psyched about each of the three musicians scoring the film, the three versions of the film. You know for now I'm sworn to secrecy as to the other folks. You were there when we saw the two versions of *Contempt* with different scores screened in adjacent theaters. We'd watch some of the one with the Delerue and then bop next door for the Italian cocktail jazz version. I don't want to tell you what to do because I'm confident that these three scores will be altogether different, and these will turn out to be three distinct films. When I first went to Bolivia to shoot I couldn't think straight; it took longer than I'd imagined to acclimatize. Still, I knew that there could be no single score matched to the salt flats. I didn't want to squander, I didn't want to settle, and I don't want you to settle. I'm not sure how any of this gets expressed musically. I don't want to tell you how to do your work, but I'm giving you this pep talk because I don't want you to fuck it up and even Studio B isn't cheap. I hope you're enjoying your snowy getaway. I also hope you can finish the tracking and a rough mix in a day's time because that's our agreement. You did fine on the last one, and this can't be anything like it. This one has nothing to do with architecture or social spaces, nothing to do with churches or anything resembling worship. I couldn't tell you where the nearest church might be. The crucial thing is not the pickup truck as it approaches the vanishing point. It's not the time spent waiting after the pickup leaves you behind, as it tries to exit the scene of salt and sky, salt and sky and tire tracks only, with you left standing there or flat on your ass helpless. It literally makes tracks. Extremely long ones. You're flat on your ass on the hardpacked salt, or in a theater, or at home watching a screen of who knows what size, but eventually the pickup truck does merge with the single pixel. The truck disappears into the landscape, is swallowed up by, is contained within the vanishing point, or within each set of eyes' own vanishing point. There really is such a place; there's a multitude of such places. Just when you think that the worst has come to pass, that the pickup is gone for good, that it left you behind and disap-

peared, that it to all intents dematerial-
ized and there's not a soul in sight nor is
there likely to be any time soon, just then
there's the tiniest experience of a surface
disruption, the next-to-invisible distant
pulverizing and scattering of hard-packed
salt. How far can a person see? How far
can a rifle shoot? I picture a bullet run-
ning out of gas and falling to the ground.
The worst is not the disappearance of the
pickup truck that left you there, it's that
tiny irruption affecting the topography
of nearly the flattest spot on the planet.
It's the small distant cloud of salt and ex-
haust that emerges from the vanishing
point, that agglomerating molecule of
pixels. We watch the cloud mushroom,
and what you see at the distance of more
than a mile is the smallest evidence of a u-
turn. They've forgotten something, and
now they're coming back for it. Maybe
they're coming back for you — everyone
will have their own theory. The vehicle
grows in size, without a doubt it's return-
ing, it's headed toward the viewer, it pre-
sents a challenge to the viewer. Forget the
tragedy of being dumped in the salt flats,
stranded in the flats, this is a horror film
in which the black pickup truck is speed-
ing its way back toward you, toward all of
us. It ramps up to maximum speed, and

what had shrunk to a single pixel before vanishing now returns and is metastasizing at a terrible rate. Whatever variety of road warrior or warriors that's driving it has got to be pissed. Can you imagine passing through the vanishing point, such the dramatic exit, and then having to turn around and haul ass all the way back to where you started? I have confidence that you can get this in your score, and I don't really think you're the Squanderer, which isn't to say that I don't think that you're talented. If I were a composer or musician and the pickup was coming at me across the salt flats I might imagine an inverse dynamic such that as the pickup truck grows from pixel to speck to murderous nemesis the score and the location sound conversely decline in intensity, nearly disappear, just as a soul in danger blots out everything except for the most urgent threat. The blue cloudless sky and white salt flats with gray vanishing lines and angel of death pickup paralyze the ears at the final instant as the truck grows insanely to fill the screen and then disappears, hurtling past us one and all, leaving behind the white band and the blue band and the triangle of lines converging at the horizon. Because that's the first shot of the film.

After the conversation is finished and the filmmaker clicks off, the engineer begins to download the video file of the final edit, which at this point lacks only the musical score

or one of three scores, and the final sound mix for each version will be undertaken at a later date under the filmmaker's supervision. With the exception of the soundtrack, all of the audio materials for the film are present in this final edit in a rough mix of location recordings from Salar de Uyuni and elsewhere that the musician—each of the three geographically dispersed musicians—is free to use as befits her or his purpose. The musician has lived with images of the salt flats for more than a year, first in the form of snapshots and videos sourced online, later with gorgeous production stills and the longstanding, ultimately honored promise of unedited footage described in the course of numerous telephone skull sessions.

For years the musician has been a go-to for sounding gaps in the map.

———

Lean inward from the border. Set your back to it.

Start from the seam and fingertiptoe toward the printed designation "Unknown Regions." Spread out and reorient the map, shift the object of scrutiny so that the lacuna becomes the center

around which names of cities and towns cluster. What happens in Zones 1 and 2? The video footage suggests that it's monitored and mined by machines. On the basis of what we're shown, no humans are present. Shadowy packs of animals orbit fences presumed to be humming with electricity.

Among the scenes previously scored by the musician: aerial footage around and above an enormous, depopulated but nonetheless productive mining complex; a remote, far-north fishing village out of season captured in the deep cadences of its inhabitants; and a single shot rendered in extreme slow motion showing the act of removing a coat that under a time microscope abandons its owner, flouts gravity, morphs into

bird of prey pinioned in domestic space

diving for the kill, unnoticed

except by terrorized audiences. There's also the film that depicts a journey from rush-hour megacity subway hub to regional train station to the end of the line, then a bus to the end of its line, and then a significantly smaller and more crowded bus to the end of another line, the camera finally disembarking

to explore the grasslands of a convincing middle of nowhere until the sequence runs in reverse, retracing steps and bus rides and train and subway trips all while engaging in a complement of mirror-image encounters and conversations amid a sparseness of musical cues.

All good gigs. Then there's the present one

two dissimilar halves of a twenty-minute span torqued into an arc of audiovisuality through the responses of three composers. Three separate arcs, three separate films. The fact of being in the dark about the identities of the other composers weighs on the musician. His concern isn't that of competing for the most brilliant or most elegant or wildest solution; it's his fear of the three scores' received-wisdom sameness, an interchangeable also-ran emptiness

the transposability of objects

in a field. He decides to start the next phase of his workday —a hike—on snowshoes furnished by Skylight Recording.

———

Exterior view with the Squanderer.

Nor is the musician happy about his new name. The first time that the filmmaker insisted on coming up with one, years earlier, had to do with her being broke but wanting to give him a birthday present—hence the gift of the honorific "Superadequate," which mercifully did not catch on. In the language of real estate, better than it needs to be.

Better than one needs to be, the pathos.

Winter quiet amplifies the faintest room tone

of one's own, packs those doubts as baggage, and brings them as close as the ringing in your ears. The musician on the snowy hillside mulls a distant dissatisfaction at being the composer of depopulated vistas and extreme flyovers. He reasons that by playing his part in picturing remote locations his contributions affirm viewers

in maintaining their distance. The film of the seemingly uninhabitable becomes the pleasurable projection of a life of renunciation deferred, the persistent option that almost everyone lower-case squanders. As regards leaving it all behind snowshoes are a start. Viewed from the south, from its driveway and main entrance, Skylight Recording is a low-slung single story of Prairie modernism curiously absent from architectural histories, a rectilinear pile of slab-like stones marked with a later owner's touches of dark orange and pale blue. On a day such as this the orange trim detaches itself from the disappearing bulk of building and creates an illusion of floating Flavinesque forms out in the woods. There but for fortune

go a number of backwoods retreat recording studios formerly of the first rank. Skylight's success at keeping its doors open contrasts with its onetime closest competitor from just a state away, the former ski lodge of a family of Midwestern beer royalty. Between owners the competing studio's operations ceased, and while it lay fallow in spread-

sheets of real-estate speculation the hardiest of a small stand of trees grew through its windows and into the attic, eventually piercing its crumbling roof. Totemic flexing of baddest spirits yet encountered

keeping watch over these woods. These trees of legend were organizing principle and exhibit A in a resurgent ecosystem with squirrels, rats, raccoons, and meth users taking up residence while rotting shag sprouted new life.

Crunch frozen snow, a wonderfully harsh spectrum of sound. Attempt to regularize breathing. Try to do so perfectly in an effort to align with the pulse of the afternoon. Vague scrutiny of an absence of tracks culminating in unshoveled outlines of two or three cars: waveforms.

At the west end of the building an elevated walkway supported by a sheaf of two-story orange metal stilts terminates in an octagonal glass porch. A Face sleeps

beneath a splayed book. Trace the building's outline and skirt the dramatic falling away from hill to stream to innocuous Birnam Wood. A series of sliding glass doors along the north side frames by means of orange and blue rectangles a fogged-in swimming pool with another solitary Face. Next is the two-story living room and its enormous stone fireplace emblazoned with the grandest of the studio's many double pine-tree motifs, followed by the live room of the smaller of the two recording studios, the one to which the musician will soon return. Studio A fans out windowlessly to the south in the form of a bulging black shuttlecock tail.

The musician avoids getting lost only by keeping the potentially fugitive structure in his sight at all times. We should add a voice

he explains to the engineer as he struggles to remove the snowshoes and jacket and layers of clothing that hamper the effort. I'd like to try a handful of voices in a handful of rooms with a range of microphones, and I'll reserve judgment until I've heard them all. We might try using the zither as a miniature reverb chamber. I'll attach a contact mic and tune it to my voice if the instrument can be made to hold pitch.

Halo the singing stowaway. Tune it to the trunk, tune it to the interstate beneath. The musician starts in the vocal booth, clearing out piles of cardboard boxes so that he'll have enough room for stretches to full wingspan and calisthenics that bring him to an audible edge of breathlessness. It's too late in the game to take up smoking again, to coat or by coughing roughen, to semiparalyze his vocal cords.

Face the mic. Draw a bead on the silver capsule

nested within black matte metal mesh. Meditate on a dull beacon further dulled by the placement of the windscreen. Take a shallow whiff of windscreen. Shift your stance, alter your gaze to actively play the interference pattern. Fine-tune the moiré, snort at the screen. Center yourself and note the exact placement of your feet, toes just so, for you'll likely need to regain that precise mark. The distance of a dollar bill thwarts proximity effect. Get ready for the voice in the head-phones, for your own voice in the headphones singing I hear myself singing with the slightest delay, testing ga ga ga, ra ra, oo. Oo oo and a suctiony pop against the roof of the mouth, a tsk and comparable consonant clusters, low pleading moans accompanied by two bars of

finger snaps, and a blurt of reputable vocalese

bottoming out below his range

completes the thought. The musician oscillates his face with
ludic variable speed the better to comprehend the micro-
phone's axis. At what point in the head's swivel does the voice
fall away? A slow approach toward the edge of the pickup
pattern tames sibilance and lends a darkness that suits the
softest of sighs. Lean back, revel in that improvised side-to-
side tremolo, get good and wild and dizzy, and feel the voice
as it disappears from the headphones yet still vibrates throat
and chest in an unamplified purr. The musician's mic check
and vocal warmup veer toward increasing abstraction and
intimacy as he grinds away with grunts and coos and disci-
plined, athletic intakes of breath. He gets sidetracked with
saliva production and wetness of tone, kid's play musical
modulation; the pilot undergoes High-G training with his
mouth at its widest in the

centrifuge of his refusal to breathe.

Strangulated sounds command attention. Adjust wind-scream. The musician's gasps and sighs and animalistic tokens of pleasure could be revisited as future musical material

were he not graying out and undergoing extremes of tunnel vision. A rapid succession of clicks in his headphones, the clearing of a disembodied throat, and the ambient hum of the control room startle the musician, putting him on notice that the engineer has been privy to these excursions into gargling and choking and sounding from deepest within. The floodlights are switched on. The musician catches his breath and confirms that all is well—he's fine, just fine—and that he's ready to approve the selection of microphone. He feels loosened up and ready to try a take, although a shift in his demeanor suggests something has been dislodged.

Where is the friction

and where's the counterforce?

The studio's absence of audience is never so palpable as when facing a vocal mic. The challenge is to improvise the counter-weight, for each individual to define his or her own threshold and release. Studio is to your

satisfaction. Often regrettably.

Studio is the absence of pushback.

Studio can be brutally low-

stakes, even as fear

of god begins

at home

.

Try to summon the terror of the first recording session. To recall, to experience again the awful uncertainty coloring every aspect of it except laying it down, killing it, which is the only thing that continues to matter

but how was one to know? Who cared what might strike a listener ten or twenty years down the line? On its maiden voyage a raft of teenagers powered through the all-important set list, that mnemonic meta-composition of songs in the sequence in which they were written and imagined appearing on record: the debut album as chronology. Once in the studio, everything did in fact go down first or second take, and after an hour they'd earned a side break.

That recording session marked a first time on the clock and a first concern about who knows how we're going to pay for this, even at a softspoken hippie's cut-rate basement studio sourced from the Yellow Pages, way out past the suburbs, the vocal booth a nook shoehorned beneath the stairs in which the singer freaks out and strips off his clothes just when the studio owner's jazzer friends stop by and ask you cats in the union?

Do you mind cranking up the level?

This is going to be a quiet take, and I need to hear the audio from the rough cut of the film, the location sound. The musician controls the headphone mix via portable console, helping himself to a combination of the filmmaker's field recordings and the Familiar Faces' electronic percussion while muting the organ, feedback guitar, and boombox recording from the trunk. The dial at the far right controls the volume of the live vocal, and the musician raises it to a level such that a sixty-cycle hum gloomily subtends. A solitary bounce of the headphone cord against his shirt violently cuffs his ears, putting even this accomplished masochist on notice.

Obedient, bodily hypercognizant, ready to—

You're rolling.

The musician leans into the windscreen and delicately scrapes his cheek against the nylon that's meant to stop pops. Exhales, deadened plosives, and a basso continuo of rubbing—skin, clothing, anything close at hand—contribute to the vocabulary of the performance. Combine with gulps of air from holding one's breath too long plus a smidge of the quietest singing in the world

the quietest yet captured on this snow-covered planet. It's the dawn of and maybe the final example of. Principled restraint and extravagantly delicate singing communicate an injunction against voices in their everyday array. The potentially deafening volume in the headphones is key to a controlled situation that restricts and compels song, deposes under duress—self-imposed—and provides a measure of pushback. The musician settles into sustained tones free of bending or shading.

At some point in the take he revisits a concert of contemporary music attended as a teen during which he ought to have paid more attention to the burlap sack at the edge of the stage. As the orchestra's gravid listlessness swelled to full-force lurching, the bag began to convulse, struggled to an upright position, and without warning fell harmlessly to the ground

as a soprano shed her confines. Had she been singing all the while?

After the singer emerged, she took control and the composition coalesced; the moderately disdained performance assumed an entirely different aspect and slayed the teen, and now these many years later he has cause to recall it in the midst of a take. His own first vocal pass requires ten slag-heaping minutes to wriggle out of the bag to produce a modest portion of song, a simple one

full of pauses for refocusing. Best to dispose of the introductory rubbing and heavy breathing and isolated stopped consonants. The musician makes a jotting in the notebook that tallies takes and helps to prepare for the mix. But first to the granite room for another pass. The engineer complies, and the two of them lug gear to Studio B's most distant isolation room, an eccentric pentagonal chamber cladded with locally quarried dimension stone. The walls are cool to the touch, and the musician sets up where he can spread his arms with both palms pressed against rock. Tired Samson should rest

and promises not to bring down the temple. With this second effort he begins musically where he left off, the difference being that for the first several minutes he shies away from directly confronting the microphone. His singing savors and explores the off-axis coloration; he listens for air and stone and touches of compression that flatter the singer and ask for more. He's wise to the closed-circuit seduction of performer as listener as performer, and chooses instead to inhabit each tone as a destination, ensuring the uniqueness

of every span of silence. By choosing to sing—really to sing—from the top of this second take he's flipped the structure, deciding that the ten-minute shot of the salt flats with the disappearing and reappearing truck might only require the location sound and this one voice singing of

visible limit and distant edge. His improvisation is scripted to the extent that it foreshadows the appearance in the second half of the film of a second voice, an entwining with the quietly sung part of the preceding take together with some combination of the day's stockpiled musical resources.

Automatic singing is the dream.

Automatic song worth the singing

the dream you dream your life about.

What is there in the image to echo against?

For now leave sound and picture unzipped, just the one voice with gentle slapback and darkened timbre as counterpoint to sky and blinding white flats. Nod to a wizened director who proposed in a newspaper interview two distinct versions of a film he admired but whose score he found impossibly apt

one mutes the sound, one abolishes the image.

———

What do you mean you haven't started mixing? Oh. That's my mistake about the time change. It's the middle of the night here, but I'm only eight hours ahead, and you're the night owl, so I'll quit my hovering. When do I get to hear something? I guess I can't just be hanging out over here in the corner minding my own business in surveillance mode. I didn't think so. We can talk about the new edit of the film if you like, although I don't want to slow you down. Wait, how is it that you've finished tracking when you haven't watched the final edit? Is that how it works? That's not the sort of thing I'm supposed to know. Besides, the second half of this new version is substantially different from what you last saw. I think it's fair to say that you hardly know a thing about it. You don't know anything about its rhythm, because that's now my department, my new department. In the second half of the film I've taken charge of the rhythm and it's a whole different game, one for which I'm not sure that you're prepared, and I won't have you clashing with it. I'm genuinely warning you. I've got to be fierce about this new department of rhythmic sensibility.

What the musician marvels at most about the filmmaker is her willingness to change her mind at the last moment. He's certainly seen it, lived it—everything hinges on the last in an accelerating sequence of decisions, a phone call from Havana

or a final deck-clearing spasm. It's hard for the musician to know what these late-in-the-game recalibrations on project after project feel like for the filmmaker. There's pride in the extremity of gesture, in decisiveness and finality, and a sheer contrarian rush in neutralizing presumptions about working collaboratively. The two have traveled some distance since they were last in the same room: an episode in which they sat at opposite ends of a nearly empty theater, an expensive rental and a disastrously planned last-minute screening, sometimes

it doesn't come together and sometimes the last-second decision proves ridiculous. The filmmaker's technique for dealing with the horror of the screening involved hiding behind sunglasses and blasting on headphones an incongruous alternate soundtrack to mask the musician's, passing the time humming and drumming in the back row, allowing garbled exhortations to percolate into shouts, and periodically stomping up and down the aisle to cast aspersions on her own film. Shitty afternoon.

But now it's evening. Irradiate snow-fort studio.

A rough mix needs to happen before Skylight Recording
shuts for the night. To luxuriate in the studio is altogether
relative, and given the right conditions—the right task—a
few hours can count as the grandest, most generous expanse
of time. Sing sliding scales

no luxury like pacing yourself in the homestretch.

The auditioning of individual tracks is the dumbest and most satisfying of remixes, the examination of one strand at a time. It can seem the truest drama that unfolds in the studio: patient inspection

and what arises. The louder the clock ticks the more determined the musician is to weigh all the things that could be, to give the time of day to each riotous impulse. The placement and handling of every fragment is assessed according to criteria that are fleeting

but nonetheless strongly felt, even if impossible to reconstruct. The musician's hometown acquaintances have begun showing their Faces again in the control room, casually appearing with pilferings and offerings from the arsenal of instruments in Studio A. With a for-now unfailing politeness the musician declines their assistance. Filmmaker be damned, he's confident that nothing else needs to be added to the session. From here on out it's all about paring and combining from the surfeit of existing elements. The engineer sets up an additional monitor with which to view the final cut of the film, and the musician a tad ceremoniously assumes the engineer's place at the 40-channel mixing console, a most satisfying field of play.

The musician is wary of faders moving of their own accord. His first experience of console-automation uncanny—faders rising and falling under unseen hands—took place one Saturday afternoon in Maida Vale years before; each channel unexpectedly came to life and pursued its own ant-like logic

the spell broken only by the producer's request that the group decamp to the canteen so he could start the mix. A couple of decades down the line and automation takes place in the box via virtual pencil: drawing, dragging, scrubbing, scumbling, and all the techniques of waveform mountaintop removal. The process retains none of the real-time team effort that once characterized the execution of an especially complex mix during which everyone lends a hand and prays that this will be the one.

The ideal sixties fade plunges

down the rabbit hole, accelerates toward zero.

The final edit of the film has been synchronized with the day's multitrack recording, the whole slew of stabs at generating material. It's astonishing what one forgets in the course of not so many hours of concentrated effort. In this case it's the ring-modulated feedback guitar with which the musician began the session. How wrong it would be to combine the misbegotten optimism of that top-of-the-morning take with the first half of the film. What seems necessary to avoid is any attack that would identify the source as an electric guitar, that holdover from how many generations' earliest efforts at making music, poor abused tool adapted and prepared and in theory excited by everything from power drill to battery-powered fan beribboned with floss.

What's electricity when you've been abandoned

on the salt flats and lined-up in the crosshairs?

The musician pauses at the perspectival meanings of electronic sound and vanishing point, tones bending this way and that like a candle's flame, fixed pitches heard to flicker relative to a rising sine wave.

Who or what moves? Accelerate toward one

———

and negative one, splinter down

or right back up the rabbit hole. The solo guitar from the
start of the day might be something to hear by itself, but
when combined with these images it's rank tourism. The ex-
ploding amplifier could tell a different story. Consider isolat-
ing those moments of fury when glass tubes ache

to bursting. The recording from within the trunk proposes
a contrast: exterior shot of distant speeding pickup matched
with audio from inside a vehicle wired for sound. How does
the warbly unauthored recording gibe with the dazzling
sharpness of the footage, the experience of which is only
suggested in a compressed video file on a middle-of-the-road
monitor? It doesn't. A poisoned engine seizes, won't burn the
wrong stuff.

Got to hand it to the Faces. Their sparse, detourned percussion trio when whittled still further makes a promising pairing of image and sound with no particular logic to the match: no function as regards illustrating, inverting, juxtaposing, celebrating, or refusing.

No rancor and no embrace.

However ungridded and self-cancelling, the electronic percussion supplies a degree of rhythmic quirk to the first half of the film and presages the filmmaker's declared newfound sensibility—hand me your instrument—in the visual patterning of the second half. Two shades of skitter

———

one for the disappearance, one for the return, and what kind of song is that? One that even you might be able to sing.

The improvised song glints through the interstices of the percussion trio, delivered as if out of earshot: now there's a reason

to croon. For those who know what's to come, the voice is heard warming up to duet with itself, building to branching modes.

———

The second half of the film begins with a thunderous fall of darkness and a bramble of voices cautioning where not to step. Instant opaque evening

arrives with its abundance of places to hide. This half of the film is shot in a video format that's a decade or more out of date; it feels remembered or retrieved, the content above all informal. First impressions center on obsolete media and the many textures of murk virtuosity

journaling. It's a cold night on the beach and pebbles sound underfoot. This extreme change of scene jars following ten minutes of stationary camera beneath an unremitting sun. The musician and the engineer lean in toward the bounded darkness of the computer monitor, imagining the effect of a vast amplification of scale on this sequence of images when projected. Unexpected turbulence in the known world in the extant world dimly pictured as darkened beach. Human silhouettes mass in groups to drink and smoke and laugh and prop themselves against one another. Dog silhouettes dart. Everyone and their mother

is high, everyone in the world. There's a bonfire on the beach, and another, and over time glimpses of many more. The musician has previously seen an unedited version of this footage that triggered sympathetic resonances of smoke and alcohol burning

the gullet. People collide and stay that way in order to fend off ocean winds. In this final edit the filmmaker makes good on her boast of an overmastering visual rhythm. It comes at you with machine-like interpolations

textured shards of night

stuttering colorwheel of under-

lit video and seam after seam after seam

jittering around pulse atop pulse.

The person behind the camera does character

study so that face becomes bonfire

and your task is to root for its reappearance.

You and your gang collide and merge with another in search of a face. Focus efforts on that glimpse to come, the time is now to exercise your best ex post facto mind control to influence the videographer's eye and the editor's hand. Eccentric lappings of flame lend dissimilar, contradictory appearances to each individual. After several minutes of footage from the darkened beach, the blinding salt flats seem as distant as they geographically are, day and night

two feet scarcely able to touch the ground

on opposite sides of the bed. The half of the film shot on the beach opens with a minutes-long montage of faces cut to chopped rhythms, one magnetic visage after the next, clue after clue with not much else to study except fire sparks

and funked-up mismatches of video grit. The filmmaker has provided the musician with the sound of the wind and the surf captured by the camera's built-in microphone and presented as a continuous take not affected by the syncopation of images.

In time the fragments of collaged video start to breathe more freely. Shots are lingered over, the overall tempo subsides, and the rhythms of editing simplify to a point of near-transparency. When the freneticism that had marked the segment finally disappears, the camera swings a laborious 180 degrees to reveal an enormous conflagration way out near the end of the pier, comprehended in an instant as the occasion for this middle-of-the-night revelry on the cold beach. A mammoth octagonal structure is enveloped by flames and the camera takes a heartbeat or two

to regain its composure, to find

its focus. The burning building tilts an almost perfect forty-five degrees. It looks on the verge of detaching and sliding into the ocean while the blaze illuminates the metal ribs of an even larger ruined structure beyond it at the end of the pier. The filmmaker holds the shot for a minute or more with a sudden steadiness of hand.

Strangely there's no acknowledgment in the audio recording of the colossal fire near the end of the pier. Instead there's only breeze, surf, breath, feet dragged through pebbles, and an undertow of small talk. Where are the signs of alarm? The camera swings back, resumes its search for faces, and reality-checks the now comparatively small bonfires on the beach. A brief coda of quick cuts and juxtapositions of minimally differing shades of camcorder darkness together with a long fade out of the location sound bring the film to a close.

For the musician, it's hard to know what to add. The scene on the beach feels complete in itself, and the temptation is to let the evening and its repertoire of sounds slip into the sea. Let them ash into the sea. Moved by the segment's inventions, the musician considers whether the location sound, un-touched by an editor's hand, is very nearly the best solution.

But what to do with the wind

and the gusts of blown-out microphone?

Regarding the beach at night, the recording has little to do with the experience of listening to the wind. Human listening, that is, as the location recording chiefly registers the microphone's overtaxed diaphragm. There are remedies. Filters carve frequencies for better and worse, tough incisions for intransigent transients. The musician thinks to ask the engineer about outpatient options for addressing unflattering distortion

then decides that surgery is off the table. He revisits the recording's various knots of conversation, delivers sculpted boosts in volume, and starts to place found voices at the center of his contribution. Only then is he ready to add the two layers of his own voice, carefully managing entrances and exits so as to avoid traces of editing. His singing becomes singing on a beach becalmed, submerged within the crowd. There are sections in which speech from the location recording and the super-imposed passes of today's improvised song serendipitously line up, and these swells

moments within which pivots point

become the macrostructure of the score. Suddenly sanguine about thickening the plot, the musician unmutes the multi-tracked organ and introduces it into the mix. As it becomes increasingly audible the organ can't help but chomp the scenery, conspicuously snarf it, best to bring down the volume to where it's hanging out and looking handsome.

Once or twice the organ lumbers forward, checks out action that it invariably fails to comprehend, and retreats and resumes its pacing back and forth across the stereo image. Its dynamic peaks and troughs map onto the nodes of speech and song such that it alternately figures as accompanist, choir, or creature

from the pitch-black surf. It washes up on the pebbled beach only to be reclaimed by the next outward flow, and the organ's one ruminative soliloquy becomes solipsistic chatter within an especially dense fabric of sound.

The filmmaker's on the line again.

I don't know that I properly accounted for why we're on the beach. On the morning after the memorial service, I woke up having had a dream that all of us, all of the folks who had gotten up and made noise at the end of the service, that all of us as a group agreed to commit one weekend every month to get together and complete artworks that he had left unfinished. I don't know whose idea it was, but it doesn't matter because we all agreed one hundred percent in this completely excellent dream that had me fooled. One weekend a month seemed only a moderate commitment, and so the seven or eight of us were all-in without questions or hesitations. Wouldn't you want to know more about his unfinished works? The commitment to continue working on these unfinished pieces might extend for years, and the task could well outlast all of us. When the date of the first meeting finally rolls around, we gather on a beach. The first unfinished piece involves a thirty-foot pane of glass, an enormous rectangle—perilously thin glass, tremendously heavy—and we need to be able to make it stand upright in the sand. It's an extremely windy day, cold enough that we're wearing coats and gloves. The beach is deserted. I can't say that we came prepared or that we had any idea what to expect, and we don't have any tools to speak of. The giant pane of glass sways in the wind and threatens to shatter at any moment. There are no instructions, and none of us really knows what we're doing. Who came up with the idea that we could finish these pieces? No one remembers. How could we have been so foolish as to presume the authority to do so, to assume that it's the right thing to do, and that he wouldn't have been appalled by the idea? Things get left unfinished. There's nothing stopping us from meeting once monthly without this hubristic task for which we're comically ill-equipped. I say "comically" knowing that everyone is beginning to feel whatever humor there was in the situation start to wear off. We're through talking. We're here to dig in the sand and somehow to make this enormous fragile piece of glass balance upright. Everyone is bundled up because of the weather, a bunch of hooded figures on a beach, and eventually I notice—I can't tell if anyone else has noticed—that he's there among us seven or eight friends. He's working away just like everyone else. Eventually I get the feeling that everyone has been playing it cool for some time, not making too big a deal about his pres-

ence, as if too direct of an acknowledg-
ment would force him to flee. Each of us
keeps it on the down low, only occasion-
ally saying things like "we missed you so
much." Tears are definitely not allowed.
He laughs, but never speaks. There's only
eye contact and laughter at pantomimed
misunderstandings. Intense upwellings
of emotion subside into serene afternoon.
At the end of a long, relaxed, lazy day of
"work," we understand that with his par-
ticular genius he wrangled a deal with
god knows whom according to which he
gets to return once a month to finish
these artworks. We get it that he'll be
taking his time, that he doesn't give a rat's
ass about finishing things, and that all of
this only nominally has to do with art.
Art's the excuse, the most plausible expla-
nation to be with friends. Eurydice pro-
poses a monthly furlough on her — on
his — own recognizance, and it proved
crazy enough to work. I had forgotten
about the beach footage until after the
memorial service, or until after this
dream of the plan to meet once a month,
and the beach location rang a bell that
wouldn't stop. There I was digging to the
bottom of the storage space, looking for
the beach footage that it brought to
mind. Once I had found the tape, I liter-

ally held my breath for the duration of the transfer, who knew what would happen, and I was afraid to jinx it. I put it off for a week, and then another, and in the end the transfer was flawless. The video is from 2003. We'd been walking down the beach late, well after midnight, ready to cash in our chips. It was the beginning of May but still surprisingly cold, and all around us people were totally wasted. Everywhere you looked people were colliding with one another. It was like when pubs used to close at ten and the streets would be empty at five 'til and then by five after there'd be out and out brawls, someone always stretched out and bleeding as a line of people step over him to get on the bus. We expected that the beach would be empty, but it turned out that everyone had come out to watch the pier burn. Actually it was the concert hall that was on fire, a Victorian landmark, and when we arrived it was tilted like a jaunty hat. There was no question of trying to put it out, they were just letting it burn. It wasn't the Hindenburg, but it wasn't nothing. By the light of the fire you could see what had been another enormous building at the end of the same pier, which now was just a bent iron skeleton. People explained that the ruin at the end of the pier was the pavilion, what had once been the grander of the two buildings. It also had burned down in the middle of the night—and the next day and night—just two months earlier, so this was a repeat performance. People couldn't believe it was happening a second time, and everyone was airing all sorts of theories about the arson. It didn't catch fire all by itself, neither of them did. They'd been shut for years, decades, and there hadn't been electricity in either structure in forever. One theory had to do with seabird guano spontaneously combusting. After the pavilion burned a couple of months prior, it was widely claimed that a speedboat had been seen pulling up or pulling away around the time that the whole thing went up in flames. When the first blaze broke out it was called in to the fire department by someone identifying himself as Mr. Piers Burns. Days later Burns wrote in to the local paper saying that he had swum out with five liters of gasoline—petrol—and started the fire to protest the Iraq War. The fact that the concert hall was allowed to burn, and that the fire was happening so soon after the first one, gave the scene an aura of lawlessness, the sense that the people in charge weren't going to lift a finger. I had the dream about the monthly get-togethers on the beach not long after shooting in Bolivia, which I'd imagined to be a film unto itself, a film of a single location. When I was shooting on the salt flats I weirdly didn't think beach. I didn't think blue sky equals blue water out beyond white sandy beach, although you'd think that by staring at it long enough the mirage should have appeared. I thought about lawlessness and the geometry of the shot and ways to represent time visually, especially so that it can be comprehended in a glance: the journey to the horizon, the duration of a lap. I thought about how it feels to watch and wait, to pass the time figuring out how to quantify time passing. Seeing the truck disappear and then come barreling back is like staring at a clock from an extremely oblique angle with the second hand trundling off into the distance. I look at the salt flats footage now and I see beach. I look at the salt flats and it makes me yearn for beach. All I need is a band of blue atop a ground of white, light brown, even volcanic black. Give me some blue at the horizon and I've already placed myself there. I perpetually forget that I live in a city with many miles of beach, where I can take the subway to the beach, and that the ocean is not a thousand miles away and something I only see once every few years. It's a swipe of the Metrocard. But to shoot on the beach can have too much of a surefire effect, the associations are too strong, and that's why I'm thankful that this footage comes from the middle of the night when you can hardly see anything. Scattered bonfires and then this enormous blaze, the mother of them all. Now comes our overdue conversation about the sound of wind on a microphone. How can you hate it? You're going to make me argue that it's the best part, that you're inartistic and wrong. I'm always having to check my impulse to say the opposite with you. The fact that there are three composers and three scores and three films shouldn't be taken as a vote of no confidence, you bum. My position is that the two halves of the film belong together, one demands the other, but where will your score stand on the matter? Maybe no explanation is necessary, none requested—I withdraw the question—nor am I suggesting that the score needs to wield an explanatory force. It's the persistence of salt-flats vision and basic everyday precognition that takes us down to the beach in the middle of the night.

[0:00] All present in Skylight Recording have gathered for a start-to-finish viewing of the final cut of the film with the musician's rough mix of the soundtrack. The Familiar Faces have reunited for the screening and take their spots on the couch. At a few minutes before midnight the engineer presses the space bar, exits to the adjoining kitchen, and gently seals the door to the control room behind him.

[1:00] The nearly static image of white salt flats beneath an ultramarine sky holds firm while the musician's contribution remains in reserve. The scene resembles a photograph. Eyes from the couch

check the time display with increasing regularity. Apart from the occasional gust of wind, it's a challenge for the listeners to separate the quiet location sound from the noise floor of the playback, not to mention the inner-ear anomalies of mid-career musicians. [1:15] Even the most hearing-damaged of the lot by this point are able to distinguish the faint but steadily growing sound of an engine whose alarming, eventually room-shaking crescendo [2:00] peaks as a black pickup truck roars past the stationary camera

enters the frame from the left

and causes a violent tremor in the image it momentarily dominates. The vehicle couldn't have missed the camera and tripod by more than a few feet. White ground, blue sky, careening

black truck with license plate removed. **[2:14]** The volume decrescendo in the aftermath of the truck entering the frame reveals a solitary pitch held by a voice until it runs out of breath. **[2:28]** A handful of clunky attacks of electronic percussion scatter in the silence following the sung tone, pinging mechanical adjuncts to the gunned engine; the Familiar Faces recognize their contribution and brighten considerably. **[2:51]** A second sung pitch held for the duration of a breath is answered by **[3:04]** another arrhythmic cluster of poks and dut duts, proof of an emerging musical logic. Everyone can relax.

[4:00] Cousin: Is that the end? It looks like the last shot of a film.

[4:45] For the viewers at the back of the control room, attention drifts away from a soundtrack that has reliably settled into a broad-stroked pattern of call and response, one that shades quieter and more sparse as the fleeing vehicle becomes smaller and smaller. Depending on one's eyesight and proximity

to the computer monitor **[c. 5:25]** the truck finally shrinks to invisibility, the three viewers on the couch startled to varying degrees at the moment of its perceived disappearance. In place of the truck a small cloud of dust remains, represented by progressively fewer and fewer gray pixels. The electronic percussion and the voice have ceased, not arriving at a musical conclusion but rather after a long rest failing to report for duty. Once the cloud of dust is gone the image is for all purposes identical to the one at the start, with the exception of a set of tire tracks on a slight diagonal, tilting right and terminating at the horizon. The scene is accompanied as before by a faint hue of location sound.

[5:42] Cousin: That's the entire movie? What was that? Brother: People are always needing to leave their mark, and this is a first slash, a first defacement. The scourge of human inhabitation. Sister: Inhuman habitation. Brother: Inhuman inhabitation. Sister: Unhabitation. Brother: You can only see so far into the distance, and beyond that it's just floaters. Cousin: What's a floater? Sister: Then I guess it's on us.

[5:55] Cousin slides off the couch

hits the ground with a thud, and lies still on the floor with his knees drawn to his chest. His timing is impeccable

as the fall coincides with a distant, barely perceptible event within the image, like a whacked television brought to its senses. The event first presents as a flaw, a very small one. It's a bug in the pixel amber, a remote squall of image distortion. Blank eventless horizon becomes gray dancing speck becomes black truck hightailing it toward the viewer.

[6:01] Sister and Brother: Holy shit!

———

Cousin refuses to take the bait, won't lift his head to look at the screen. Brother: OK, that's bad. Really bad. Why are they coming back? Sister: You probably expect us to ask why you're lying on the ground. Cousin: [silence]. **[6:10]** The singing voice returns

this time noticeably louder and overlapping with a denser grouping of electronic percussion, no longer taking turns but instead joining forces and marshaling resources. The pitch of the truck's engine keens higher, the driver threatening to max out the vehicle. **[7:28]** Brother: It's amazing how long this is taking. This is super-painful. Sister: Executioner approacheth!

[7:45] A glassy rattling tops out the frequency range. The truck's engine dominates the sound mix through sheer volume but also by having been thickened with low-end feedback and the cassette recording from the trunk. **[9:00]** This complex din swallows the voice and electronic percussion, eliminates connection to music, to a decadent past

to an even older regime. **[9:21]** Sister: Moment of truth!

[9:30] The black pickup truck rushes to fill the screen, barrels to the right of the camera, causes the image to shake wildly, and continues on its way toward wherever the hell or whatever hell it was pointed, the sound now having crested and begun to subside and leaving nothing in its wake that could be mistaken for music. The cloud of dust enveloping the area around the camera—fearless naked eye—softens the scene, gives it a gauzy cast that slowly settles back into the status quo with which the film began. The only addition to the image is a pair of scissoring, miles-long sets of tire tracks. Monolithic crosshatch. Train ears on the truck's diminishing whine until

[10:00] night in an instant has long since fallen.

[10:23] Brother: Wow, this video looks like garbage.

[10:48] Sister: This editing is insane. Cousin: [silence]. The aural realization of glass-rattling, teeth-chattering terror beneath an unyielding sun has been replaced by a stoned world of layered location recordings from the darkened beach. A dulled sheen dapples fugitive conversations and lurching footsteps through pebbles.

[11:15] The rapid editing of erratically lit figures on the beach at night counterbalances the real-time, point-of-audition perspective on the scene. Drunken voices do their best

with fragments of song whoah whoah but nobody can agree on the words. A familiar voice weaves in and out of these wasted choruses.

[11:31] Sister: Is that you singing? Musician: Yes. Sister: Is it the same recording from before? Musician: No. Similar melody. Sister: Now it's two of you? Musician: Yes.

[13:52] Sister: Everyone is slowing down. Everything seems to be slowing down. The filmmaker is slowing down, the editor is slowing down. The chemicals are definitely winning. Whoever cast this is a genius. I mean, I know

no one cast this.

[15:30] Brother: Pardon me, but what *is* that? Sister: *Where* is this? Brother: Are there people inside that building? Sister: What started the fire? Brother: Was it deliberately set? Sister: No one on the beach seems to have noticed that there's an enormous building on fire. Brother: Satanic ritual. Sister: Unparalleled CGI. Brother: The *Titanic* is burning. Sister: Most people don't know that you only see a fraction of an iceberg; it's the underwater part that's on fire. Brother: The sinking of the dance hall versus the sinking of the casino. Sister: My guess is that each person in the crowd at precisely the same moment counted to three and tossed a match on the building: "they either convict us all—or none of us."

[16:00] After the camera pivots back to the crowd on the beach, the soundtrack starts to flesh out a more complex musical arrangement, one that contrasts with the relative quiet from when the burning building dominated the frame. As the score becomes busier, the multitracked organ first makes its presence felt

and then heard. Each pitch traces an arc

of its own momentum as the creaturely assemblage stirs and slowly traverses the stereo image. The Familiar Faces' electronic percussion trio returns in its most rhythmic guise, a variety of half-time and quarter-time supremely downtempo dance music neither getting this party started nor breaking it up, not hassling anyone at all.

Each pitch that's added to the organ part broadens the compass of the cluster, lets those legs stretch. The layers of mumbled conversations return, this time combined with the distant unsanctified organ and ingenious sketches of beats that come together only to collapse. Faces no longer interest the filmmaker. Pictured instead are hands, legs, feet, and the surf illuminated by fire. The final collection of images is the most dimly lit and difficult to parse, and the editing gradually begins to conform to a grid of rhythmic regularity. This short concluding section—what Cousin will refer to as the dénoumonument—consists of a linear mosaic of mismatched shades of darkened sky so that in the final moments the viewer is left only with the textures of the medium while the concert hall blazes off-screen. **[19:40]** The last element heard on the soundtrack, emerging at the end of a minute-long fade, is a loop of synthesized kick drum alternately revealed and obscured by the white noise of the waves.

[20:00] Sister: I think you've saved the film.

Insert sound of space bar being struck.

All rise, with the exception of Cousin, still sprawled on the floor. The musician looks at Sister and mouths "Protest?" to which she shrugs. On cue the door to the control room opens and the engineer enters and begins preparations for backing up the day's recordings. As he starts to tidy, the control room reverts to his domain. A stack of audio engineering magazines is straightened, couch cushions are smoothed out, lamps are turned off, glasses and coffee mugs disappear. He carefully steps over Cousin, but doesn't say a word. In the live room dimmed lights are extinguished, the glass sliding doors locked, and the curtains pulled. The engineer confirms the musician's method of payment.

Sister: Do you want to explain why you fell off the couch?

———

Cousin: [silence]. Sister: And why you're lying on the ground?

Cousin: Everyone was so concerned about what was happening a thousand miles away in a place none of us are ever going to visit. Everyone was so focused on waiting for something to happen in the movie that no one would have cared if a pickup truck had come crashing through the wall of the studio or if someone had a heart attack and fell off the couch and died.

Brother and Sister: [silence]. Cousin: Can we go swimming now?

Before adjourning to Skylight Recording's indoor pool, the musician wonders aloud if he might get a peek inside Studio A. Moments later, there they are, the engineer pulling out a janitor-sized ring of keys and selecting the three correct ones. He unlocks the door, jerks it open no more than a foot, and flips a long row of switches. The musician's first impression upon literally sticking his head inside is

AstroTurf. This, one of the storied sites from the golden age of destroying stuff—electric guitars and basses splintered, drum kits and amps toppled, piano benches and folding chairs hurled at the window to the control room however many times it takes

to get a point across. The musician imagines the door swinging shut on his neck. The floor of the gymnasium-sized space is covered by a billiard-green carpet with white dashed lines, semicircles, and penalty-box rectangles, a stylized version of multiple superimposed playing fields. There's a compulsive quadrilateral symmetry organizing the equipment—four islands of amplifiers, four abundant sprigs of mic stands, a central clover of acoustic baffles. It would be no problem to garrison a marching band or orchestra in here.

Maybe next time, Squanderer.

The long wall to the right of the entrance is a three-story library with books not for reading organized by the colors of their spines. Are they glued into place? A balcony wends its way along the other three walls, terminating in a control room above and a warren of isolation rooms below. The periphery is dotted with entrances and exits, access to halls, passageways, networks of tunnels lit by chandelier, sconce, fluorescent tube, and convenient blazing torch should the need arise to escape by river or rail or seek shelter from blast and fallout in a subterranean system of studios within studios. *We'll meet again, don't know how*

It's too much to take in—*don't know when*—too much to consider in the brief interval before the engineer reverses the gesture and one by one flips off the long row of light switches in Studio A.

———

Skylight Recording rises to the demands of the day as biosphere or bubble or protective shell—a skylight's not the sky—for the length of the lock-in. We'll see if tomorrow the roads are clear.

Clothes shed, four bodies hit the water at the same time with one mega-splash while the engineer slides open every one of the glass doors, throws open all of the windows, impatient cold air rolls in

and soon the pool area is impossibly thick with homemade fog—you can't see the distance to your fingertips—as the battle rages in earnest and snowballs strike their targets.

———

ACKNOWLEDGMENTS

The experience of working in the recording studio is also the experience of the language that surrounds and infuses the culture of the studio, and that language is the material of this poem. The first group of people to whom I owe thanks includes those who schooled me in the ways of the recording studio or underwent similar experiences as fellow classmates and initiates: Steve Albini, Bundy K. Brown, Charles Burst, Tony Conrad, Howie Gano, Douglas Henderson, Susan Howe, Clark Johnson, John McEntire, Brian McMahan, Will Oldham, Jim O'Rourke, Brian Paulson, Mitch Rackin, Taku Unami, and Britt Walford—among many others.

I'm fortunate once again to be the beneficiary of Ken Wissoker's guidance and support, as well as that of his colleagues at Duke University Press: Nina Foster, Diane Grossé, Michael McCullough, Olivia Polk, Chad Royal, Jessica Ryan, Jennifer Schaper, Laura Sell, Matthew Tauch, and Joshua Tranen. Excerpts from this book first appeared in *Hotel* and *Ear | Wave | Event*; thanks for these early airings are due to Jon Auman, Bill Dietz, and Woody Sullender.

Josiah McElheny is an artist whose invigorating responses to music, politics, and performance provide ongoing inspiration, and I'm grateful for his generosity in allowing his artwork to appear on the book's cover.

Cathy Bowman, John Corbett, Terri Kapsalis, Ben Lerner, and Amnon Wolman read this book in draft form and responded with sage, crucial advice. It also benefited from exchanges about music and writing with Drew Daniel, Lawrence English, T. R. Johnson, Eli Keszler, Lawrence Kumpf, Eric Lorberer, Petar Milat, Rick Moody, Daniel Muzyczuk, Ben Piekut, Robert Polito, Marina Rosenfeld, Jan St. Werner, M. C. Schmidt, Lytle Shaw, John Sparagana, Mónica de la Torre, Ellen Tremper, Jennifer Walshe, Julian Weber, Marjorie Welish, Krystian Woznicki, and Volker Zander. Thank you Susan and Bill Grubbs and Ruth and Roger Bowman.

This book is dedicated, with love, to Cathy Bowman and Emmett Bowman-Grubbs.